Blue Memento

Poems

Robert Carr

LILY POETRY REVIEW BOOKS

https://lilypoetryreview.blog/

ISBN: 978-1-957755-52-6

For my sister, Cyndi.

Contents

Time to plant tears, says the almanac.
The grandmother sings to the marvelous stove
and the child draws another inscrutable house.

–Elizabeth Bishop

Beyond Bea

First: air in the small space
between mouths.

Color, swirling on the palate,
my bright blue

mixed with Bea red, creates
a pure and silent hum

of violet. Out of time,
the only thing there is,

that dusk, purple.
Remembered things

seal in our colors,
recognition of lick

in smooth heat.
In this recollected place—

I float above cardinal
and barn swallow,

grasp the touch of hands,
the next, that's more.

Brown Silk Stockings

Bea dries brown silk
stockings on the shower-

rod above my bath.
They hang like wrinkled

lady legs. Between tiles,
black and peach,

I scratch some sticky
dark stuff. She sits

on the smooth edge
of the claw-foot tub.

Stockings, drying,
tickle her hair.

Cold? she asks.
Loud hot water,

scream and giggle,
my reddening legs,

her hand a whirlpool,
between them.

Bruised Babies

Outside her house
on Duke of Gloucester,

sidewalk brick has buckled.
Frilly skirts, girls

on tricycles, stumble over
heaves, bloody knees

and cry for Bea. She ignores
them, best she can—

rose girl-whines, tomboy
cries. She tosses

a Band-Aid box
out her kitchen door.

I grab a raspberry cane,
she takes the thorns

with kisses. I'm her only
grandson, bring her

a gift of rabbit pellets
in the basket of my fingers.

Wide-eyed, she names them
her black pearls.

Gagging With Bea

She turns away
to puke

in her bucket.
I pinch white puffs

on her chenille
spread, hug a blue

beach pail.
She rolls to her side,

I look in my pail
to see if I can

throw-up too.
There's not much

Bea in the bucket,
just a little spit

in mine. I press
against her thigh,

we groan in unison.
She soothes me

when we're sick—

*Moaning always
makes it better.*

Pink Kittens

Bea's second floor bathroom
hangs off the house

like a sinking boat.
She moves around the kitchen.

You know you had a brother.
She lost him,

upstairs in the bath.
Says my brother slipped out

mom into the tub—
just like a little pink kitten.

An open fridge.
She fans her summer dress,

airs coochie in the cool,
shakes a wooden box

of strawberries turned
to fuzzy mice, bends

some wilted carrots, holds
a bottle of pickled pig's

feet up to light. *What you want*
for dinner, baby?

Girl Sweat and Red Lipstick

We rake and sweep
the cat-pissed ivy in her

yard. Bristles brush
crumbled brick,

Annapolis air—a July
bowl of brown beans.

My sister wipes
her forehead, *Sweaty!*

Under a turquoise-
fringed umbrella,

Bea shifts a buttock,
dries an upper lip

with handkerchief
as if she's swallowed

cardinal lipstick.
My dear, women glow,

men perspire,
pigs sweat. My sister,

murder red and shiny
shoulder muscle.

Bea's Rainbow Tree

Christmas, a fat white pine,
stands on her card table.

Upside down umbrellas
bubble on branches,

strands of tinsel clump
in needle, rainbow Bea's

swirled ceiling. I'm in
a corner behind a chair,

there's grown-up
in the air. The living room

sneezes pine sap
and sad. On the braided

rug, my sissy Lamb
Chop waves from a blue

Tonka. I can feel
this one hating that one—

Uncle Bob talks to Bea,
in whispers. *Do you think?*

She answers, *Nothing
wrong with that boy.*

Great Grandma's Golden Frame

Late at night, she carries
a green flashlight,

grips my sticky hand,
leads me through

the bulkhead
to a webby corner.

Don't be a fool! Bea
chides when I insist

spiders in her cellar
are black widows.

A fancy frame
hangs from a nail.

(It's Bea that taught us
proper—*Beef is hung,*

man is hanged.)
At our feet, fallen

chunks of plaster.
On the wall—

a forgotten canvas
in a gilded frame,

slashed by some man
who knew

she loved it.
She whispers: *Long ago,*

that held my mother's portrait.
Isn't it pretty?

Small Hooked Things

Bea teaches me crochet,
a ball of shiny polyester

string. We're making teacups
on saucers, soft

until soaked in corn starch.
They harden like her perfect

Aqua Net. My breath
is wrapped in her

big knit sweater. I love
my row of china,

hanging little handles
on a tree. I'm smelling

flaky crust, pie
she cuts in quarters

so you never have to ask
for a second slice.

Pearl Tights

Her avocado recliner
flips out over a thread-

worn rug. My arms
stick to Naugahyde,

to folds of Bea,
as we watch Baryshnikov

soar across the screen.
Pearl tights glow

on muscled dancers.
I'm flat and hard

when she says, *Will you
look at that man's ovaries!*

I touch milk
white underarms,

point a foot, dream
of undressed twirling.

Candy Cigarettes

They've got chocolate ones
at *A&P*—and bubble gums,

El Diablo cigarillo's—but I like
Just Like Dad's the best.

White, powdery, melting
on my tongue, little red flames

brushed on the tip. They taste
like baby aspirin, orange,

but only better. I study Bea—
her *Lucky Strikes*.

In a creamsicle dress, she sits
in a funny way

when smoking under the sumac:
Fingers stiff, nails done,

elbow bent, wrist dropped back
like her butt has weight.

Smoke rises between fingers,
legs cross at the thigh.

She seems to happy
melt when blowing clouds.

I practice poses on my candy-
striped swing, chew

half the pack, rock and drift
into our special blue.

Blue Memento

I reach and place a flower
in her wide-brimmed hat.

Mosquitos catch the silence
in my throat as she sashays,

gusts lift her skirt, fabric falls
in pleats that shield skin.

This is before secrets find a name
in daisies or the nests of birds.

Look Bea, I found a robin's egg!

*

Taken by the blue, we puncture
the sky's shell with a pin,

drain white and yolk away.
I leave a trace in the soft blow

of a straw, display the empty
by my cot. Kiss and kiss

and air kiss between my body
and her mouth. The robin pulls

a worm from Bea's brown lawn.
Can I return her blue memento?

Pupils dilate, shades drawn,
and every memory is bed-wet yellow.

*

Heaven opens to a hand on my toddler
thigh, her palm just a little high

for innocence. A bathroom lamp
swings like a nod. In the tub, bubbles

scatter. Wrapped in towels, we snuggle
in the wall-cloud of our storm.

She dries my many creases,
softens lines between my brows.

Reading with Bea

After the first bomb,
a hand grenade tossed

in the bathtub by Bea,
I flee to my room,

grab the red squirt-
gun, plan my escape.

I strap pencil lead to my
back, tuck a secret

map in my sock,
like a bone. Bea and I

read picture books.
I curl, with a pillow

between us, soft
as a breast, breathe

in the sugar of her
powder. In the reading

room we search for
doors between tales,

boxes strewn everywhere,
remnants of clothing

and cousins. Nursery
rhymes rise, pink

covers chewed
by toddler teeth,

a watercolor
handprint. In Civil

War stories, strange
men are pounding.

A picture frame tilts
on a wall. Secrets

trek battlefields, tear
epaulettes from loose

spines—privates
colored bloody,

sergeants choked
in crayon. A broken dog

wades in a scribble
of black. I swing

from a branch overlooking
forgotten. Tom Sawyer

and Huck have lost limbs.
On Maryland islands,

Misty of Chincoteague,
Crayola gutted, grazes.

I draw a stick figure. He hides
in the horse's big belly.

Hookus

Not a dictionary word. I searched.
Family slang for boy parts,

something like a shame flushed cheek,
an exclamation, dirty to be

cleaned, *Wash your hookus!*
Put away your hookus! (Her voice

is diamond through an earlobe.)
Jiggly, blood-stained tighty-whities,

thumb pressed to the roof
of Bea's house. I'm guessing twisted

Yiddish, *tuchus*, ass, picked up
on Annapolis streets.

Upward pointing flesh, Baryshnikov's
pale tights, ovaries on the outside.

Mr. Bubble, gum scented;
Bubbles kids clean…

softens skin. Imperfection to be cut,
divining rod in whirlpools,

dreamscape in rooms on Duke
of Gloucester, boy without a root.

Cutting the Mole

I search Mom's
mirrored vanity,

take clippers
from the drawer

where she keeps
a baby tooth

in a bottle,
a locket

with blonde hair.
The scissors

velvet sheath
is pink. The door

is locked. Sitting
on the toilet

I turn the screw
with a chewed nail,

wrap my penis-
mole in blades.

The shag seat
cover's soft against

my bum. I squinch,
bite down, shut

silver against silver,
taste a trouble-bitten

cheek. The speck,
balanced on an edge.

Several Lovers Visit Bea

Today I'm Phil, other days
I'm Bob. Each time I enter

the room, she greets another lover.
She says some things I know,

others leave me to wonder.
Fractured window, her room

the scent of alcohol and peony.
Bea grins and pulls bruised petals.

Yesterday she had no grandson
(in her cloudy eye, I haven't been born).

Parchment skinned, she cups a lover's
stubbled chin, pulls back the sheet

to flash a bedsore. *Darling,*
you look beautiful! she says, bending

the brass hands of her watch.
Sundial shade pours through

wired glass, she greets me
for the first time, on the hour.

Interchangeable rays catch dust,
milkweed pods shaken

in beloved hands. I powder privates,
respond to endless hellos.

Maryland Crab Cakes

We pinch Wonder
in pinkie sized

bits and dry them
in a pan. Back-fin

blue crab, egg,
Worcestershire,

just a splash,
two squirts French's

mustard, cigarette
ash, Bay Seasoning.

I prop my chin
on fists, mouth

watering. In a cast-
iron skillet, we brown

yellow blobs.
I'm the only one

can pick little
crispies off crab cakes

the size of Bea's palm.
Crab meat—sweet

as secrets—She says
I got brown-buttered eyes.

Green Stamps

I slide around the back seat
of Bea's Bug. She takes

sharp corners, pulls in
Sinclair with the long neck

dinosaur, fills the tank
and gets our Green Stamps.

We've searched the Idea
Book. Bea is saving

for a set of lawn chairs
she calls elegant.

At the intersection,
men are tarring, raise

stop signs up to Bea.
Out of my way you ape!

she shouts. Down the road,
Bea points to a big car

with darkened windows.
Will you look at that?

You want that car
when you grow up?

It's hot. The stink of gas
and road tar fills the air.

I let Bea know, *I don't want*
a car, I want a driver.

Talking Sex

In Bea's lemon
kitchen, backyard

light bristles through
windows. I ask her,

What's a fuck?
She holds a Fire King

bowl the color
of mint ice cream.

*Something wonderful
we don't talk about.*

Bea adjusts her dress,
cracks five eggs

in the bowl,
stares out a window,

blue hydrangea,
scrambles with a whisk.

Who's out there?
I wonder.

Not often she
won't answer me.

Smears of Chocolate Cake

With granddaughters
in high backed chairs,

I sit by Bea. Girl faces
are smeared with chocolate

cake. She keeps a jug
of milk beside her.

A mother fills juice glasses.
Bea announces—

Girls, I was a great beauty...

She talks hair—
long enough to sit on,

midshipmen in Navy
whites lining up

to touch her. After
candles and cake,

she leans back,
pats her belly.

Fat as a tick, she says,
fat as a tick.

Glowing Like a Boy

My sister would have hated
boys much less if Bea

had liked *us* best—but
she liked me, everything

that rests between
male legs. A hand swirls

bubbles in my boyhood.
I like Bea best,

and she likes me.
My sister spins on a tire

in the yard, glows above
her boyish shadow,

laughs—t-shirt, armpits
half-mooned.

Drinking With Bea

In her pantry, a Monarch
lion roars on canned

corn never opened.
She dusts a hidden bottle,

rare vintage from a sailor
friend, *For our special party.*

My juice-glass
has a peacock stencil.

She pulls the cork.
Dead great-grandpa

fills the kitchen
with a stink.

Bird juice-glasses dry,
she curses, *Piss and vinegar!*

Bea pours soured
sweetness down her drain.

Pretty Picture Books

In Bea's house, pretty
picture books

are stacked on shelves
under the stairs.

Men with slicked-
back hair

paddle pretty women
in canoes.

The handsomest wear
bowties, sport

white collars
and straight noses.

Above, her new friend
stomps hardwood

floors. Something
smashes. In hiding,

black books shake.
Bea runs down

the hall—
wears a white silk slip.

A stray thread flutters
from her hem.

I get very small
and turn big pages.

Bea's Closet

Eye-high shoeboxes,
where twins are buried

without their feet. I try
on shadows, slip into

her red ones. Purses
on bent hooks are beaded,

tasseled. I click latches,
breath purple silk

linings scented with Bea's
whispers. Above me,

hems of dresses
are cottoned with flowers,

stitched with gold
Greek keys. She has a pretty

picture of herself wearing
that mint dress—

keeps it by her bed.
Her hair, brushed back,

is black as a high heel.
Opening sleeves

of pretty dresses, head
and shoulders wrapped

in satin pleats,
I stand in Bea's closet.

Canasta

She unfolds table legs,
face to face sets

bamboo chairs.
I shuffle her double

deck, blue and red
Bicycles, ruffle

them good, like Bea
taught me. The stack's

thick and heavy,
a brick. I deal.

One must play to win!
she says

to ghosts. I'm readied
for slaughter,

we play without
words, take two,

discard one, build
the stack. I've given up

Queens, she throws
her black threes,

then freezes me out
with a deuce.

So many cards, one-
eyed Jack staring back.

She smiles when I
put down the four

I've been saving.
Maybe I'm safe,

but usually, a grin
means I'm dead.

Aqua Radio

There's a picture—
an Ocean City vacation.

Bea preens beside me
on a deck

with water view,
hair tinted blue,

the hue, somewhere
between bay

and sky. I'm a skinny
thing, dark hair

tucked behind big
ears, teen nipples

swollen, bug-bites.
She stands under

my armpit, cool
hand tucked around

my waist. We pose.
An aqua radio

on a glass-top
table—Bea listening

as Orioles
play baseball.

In Tassels

For my fourteenth birthday,
crazy aunt Sis gives me

a tasseled brown suede
vest. My sister shimmies

in jeans and cowboy boots—
she's growing breasts,

at twelve. We dance
for Bea. In her big recliner,

she says one word,
Hussy. My strips of leather

swing like a skirt when
spinning to The Doors.

The Changing Table

Water runs hot baby pink,
whoosh and kitchen sink.

Bea holds me to a diapered shoulder,
I—too young to pleasure words,

am heavy headed above
her foaming graywater. Pruned,

wrinkly, fingers cradle me in palms.
I slide away, fat-bubbled.

Twist it, please, your little lamb-
chop, wiggling on a changing table.

Look to tea-brown eyes,
It's me, Bea! The bath contains

galaxy spirals, cut flesh rosies
smeared in blue of night.

Beside the sink, I'm powdered,
squished through kneading

hands, a woman feeding.
Change me, touch me.

Wrapped in Bea's hibiscus apron,
toothy, I cling and coo.

She rocks love's buttery globes,
keeps Mom out of the yellow kitchen.

Cup it here, hard hook-us along
fingers scrubbing pucker—

soaping, sure it's clean, dressed
in sailor's suit for handing off to Mom.

Acknowledgments

The author would like to thank the journals in which the following poems appeared, some in different forms or with different titles:

Evening Street Review: "Small Hooked Things"
Exit 7 Literary Magazine: "Aqua Radio", "Maryland Crabcakes"
Former People: A Journal of Bangs and Whimpers: "Several Lovers Visit Bea"
Lily Poetry Review: "Blue Memento"
Mom Egg Review: "Pearl Tights"
Nixes Mate: "Hookus"
Ran Off with The Star Bassoon: "Beyond Bea"
Slipstream: "Brown Silk Stockings"
Third Wednesday: "Green Stamps"
Up the Staircase Quarterly: "Great Grandmother's Frame", "Talking Sex"

About the author

Robert Carr was born in Annapolis, Maryland, in 1959. He is a graduate of Bates College in Lewiston, Maine where he studied philosophy and was an active member of the Bates Dance Ensemble. Following his undergraduate work, Robert moved to Portland, where he pursued a brief career in the arts as an actor with the Children's Theater of Maine.

In 1984, Robert moved to Boston, volunteered with the AIDS Action Committee, and became the first HIV testing counselor with the Massachusetts Department of Public Health. In response to the HIV pandemic, Robert engaged in a 33-year career in public health and recently retired from the position of Deputy Director for the Bureau of Infectious Disease and Laboratory Sciences in Massachusetts.

Robert is the author of *Amaranth*, published by Indolent Books, two full-length collections published by 3: A Taos Press— *The Unbuttoned Eye* and *The Heavy of Human Clouds,* and *Phallus Sprouting Leaves,* winner of the 2024 Rane Arroyo Chapbook Series at Seven Kitchens Press. A Pushcart and Best of The Net nominated poet, Robert's work has appeared in many journals and magazines including *The Greensboro Review, Lana Turner Journal, The Massachusetts Review,* and *Shenandoah.* His website is robertcarr.org